CURSIVE PRACTICE SHORT STORIES EDITION

Writing Book for 3rd Grade
Children's Reading & Writing Books

BABY PROFESSOR
EDUCATION KIDS

Speedy Publishing LLC

40 E. Main St. #1156

Newark, DE 19711

www.speedypublishing.com

Copyright 2017

Hi Kids!

Let's practice writing cursive!

A FRIEND IN NEED IS A FRIEND INDEED

Once upon a time there lived a lion in a forest. One day after a heavy meal. It was sleeping under a tree. After a while, there came a mouse and it started to play on the lion. Suddenly the lion got up with anger and looked for those who disturbed its nice sleep. Then it saw a small mouse standing trembling with fear. The lion jumped on it and started to kill it. The

mouse requested the lion to forgive it.
The lion felt pity and left it. The mouse
ran away.

On another day, the lion was caught
in a net by a hunter. The mouse came
there and cut the net. Thus it escaped.
There after, the mouse and the lion
became friends. They lived happily in
the forest afterwards.

Once, a wolf was very hungry. It
looked for food here and there. But it
couldn't get any. At last it found a
loaf of bread and piece of meat in the
hole of a tree.

The hungry wolf squeezed into the
hole. It ate all the food. It was a
woodcutter's lunch. He was on his way
back to the tree to have lunch. But

he saw there was no food in the hole, instead, a wolf.

On seeing the woodcutter, the wolf tried to get out of the hole. But it couldn't. Its tummy was swollen.

Can you imagine what happened next?

The Oak tree always thought that he was far stronger than the reeds.

He said to himself "I stand upright in storm. I don't bend my head in fear every time the wind blows. But these reeds are really so weak."

That very night blew a storm and the mighty oak tree was uprooted.

"Thank goodness!" sighed the reeds, "Our way is better. We bend but we don't break."

THE PEACOCK AND THE CRANE

One day a peacock met a crane and said, "So sorry for you. You have so dull feathers. Look at the fine colors of my feathers."

"Well!" replied the crane, "yours do look brighter than mine. But whereas I can fly high up into the sky. All you can do is to strut about on the ground."

Once the Sun and the Wind happened
to have a quarrel. Both of them claimed
to be stronger. At last they agreed to have
a trial of strength.

"Here comes a traveller. Let us see
who can strip him of his cloak?" said
the Sun.

The Wind agreed and did choose to
have the first turn.

He blew in the hardest possible way.

As a result, the traveller wrapped his
cloak even more tightly around him.
Then it was the turn of the Sun. At
first he shone very gently. The sun went
on shining brighter and brighter. The
traveller felt hot.
Before long he took off his cloak and
put it in his bag.
The Wind accepted his defeat.

REWRITE THE SHORT STORY.

A rat and its big family were living in a baker's shop. They scraped the buns and cakes in the bakery.

The baker tried his best to put an end to the nuisance of the rats. But all were in vain. At last he brought their real enemy the cat to solve the problem.

In the very next day the cat got some tiny rats for its breakfast. The rat family

got worried about the loss of their dear ones.

They arranged a meeting They looked for an idea to escape from the cat. In the end, they decided to bell the cat.

Then one of the elder rats asked them, who is willing to bell the cat? Nobody said yes.

Instead they kept quiet.

There was an old owl that lived in
an oak. Everyday he saw incidents
happening around him. Yesterday he
saw a boy helping an old man to carry
a heavy basket. Today he saw a girl
shouting at her mother. The more he
saw the less he spoke.

As he spoke less, he heard more. He
heard people talking and telling stories.
He heard a woman saying that an

elephant jumped over a fence. He also
heard a man saying that he had never
made a mistake.

The old owl had seen and heard about
what happened to people. Some became
better and some became worse. But
the old owl had become wiser each and
every day.

There lived a black sheep in a nearby village. Every spring, he shaved his black wool and sold it to the villagers. The villagers made sweaters and socks from his black wool.

One day, the black sheep noticed that he had some more wool left. He thought, "It would be such a waste if nobody wants to buy the wool."

That afternoon, an old man came

over to his wooden shed to see him. He

wanted one bag full of the black sheep's

wool. Then an old woman came over.

She also wanted a bag full of wool. A

short while later, a little boy arrived.

He also wanted one bag full of wool.

Therefore, the black sheep prepared three

bags full of wool for them. He was

happy that all of his wool was sold off.

REWRITE THE SHORT STORY.

One afternoon, a little boy had lost his puppy. He looked under his bed. He looked all over his house. But still there was no puppy. Finally, he looked for his puppy in the garden. After a few hours, he still could not find the puppy.

The little boy was tired and was about to give up. Then he saw his neighbour, Mrs Hardin.

"I beg your pardon, Mrs Hardin. Is

my puppy in your garden?" asked the

little boy.

"Oh yes, she is. She is chewing on a

mutton bone," replied Mrs Hardin.

The little boy climbed the fence and

saw his puppy chewing on a mutton

bone. He was so happy that his puppy

was not lost but had only gone to his

good neighbor's house to eat.

BETTY BOTTER

One day, Betty Botter wanted to bake a cake. She bought some cheap butter to bake it. But something was wrong with the butter.

"This butter is bitter," said Betty Botter as she tasted the butter.

"If I put it in my cake batter, it will make the batter bitter. But if I put a bit of better butter that would make my batter better."

So, she went off to buy a better butter than her bitter butter. She mixed a bit of better butter into her cake batter. She tasted the batter and was happy that the batter was not bitter.

She adopted the best way to solve the problem. Because there will be always one.

REWRITE THE SHORT STORY.

One fine morning, a hunter was getting ready to go hunting. Before departing, he went to see his little baby. His baby was awake in a baby crib. He looked at his baby's blanket and thought the blanket might not be thick enough for the coming winter.

"Bye, my little baby. Daddy is going hunting. Daddy is going to fetch some

rabbit skin to make you a new blanket,"

said the hunter to his baby.

He kissed his baby and went off hunting.

After the hunting, he made a blanket

which saved his child from the severe

winter that followed.

REWRITE THE SHORT STORY.

Georgie Porgie was a cheeky little boy.
He liked to tease people especially little
girls.
One afternoon, he went to the park
near his house. He found a little girl
and tried to kiss her. The girl cried and
sobbed because she did not like Georgie.
Then, some boys came to the park
and saw Georgie chasing after the girl.
They shouted and laughed loudly at

Georgie. Georgie stopped chasing the
girl and ran away feeling embarrassed.
Thereafter Georgie hesitated to play with
his friends because he remembered his
embarrassment that he faced in front of
his friends. This incident prohibited him
from chasing girls thereafter.

REWRITE THE SHORT STORY.

The cows used to eat hay from the manger. One day a herd of cows came to the manger to eat hay. They saw a dog lying on the hay in the manger.

One of the cows pleaded, "Please, will you get up! We are hungry. We have to eat our hay". The dog did not take heed of it.

Once again another cow pleaded, "Please,

let us have our hay". The dog snarled
and the cow stepped back.

A wise cow ran up to the bull and
told him the matter.

The bull came and requested, "Get out,
please! Let them have their food". There
was no reply. The bull became angry.
He bellowed loudly and stamped his
legs. The dog got frightened and ran for
his life.

THE DOG AND THE DONKEY

There lived a dog and a donkey in a house of a rich man. The dog guarded his house and the donkey carried loads for him.

It was a hot afternoon. The dog was sleeping under the shady veranda. There was some noise outside. The dog just lifted up his head and went back to sleep.

The donkey asked, "Why don't you bark. It could be thieves". The dog replied,

"Mind your own business". But the donkey would not listen. He wanted to save his master from thieves. He started to bray. The master who was sound asleep got mad at the donkey the donkey and came running out with a stick. There were no thieves but it sure would have scared them off if there were!

THE DONKEY IN LION'S SKIN

A donkey dressed itself in a lion's skin. Whenever he went near the other animals and villagers they feared him. Everyone thought that he was a real lion. Soon he became bold. But one day some farmers heard him braying. They ran after him with sticks. They chased him off and told him to never come near the village again. Thus, the poor donkey paid the price for his foolishness.

THE GREEDY LION

It was a hot summer day. A lion
was feeling very hungry.

He came out of his den and searched
here and there. He could find only a
small hare. He caught the hare with
some hesitation. "This hare cannot fill
my tummy" thought the lion.

As the lion was about to kill the hare,
a deer ran that way. The lion became
greedy. He thought, "Instead of eating

this small hare, let me eat the big deer".
He let the hare go and went behind the
deer. But the deer had vanished into the
forest. The lion now felt silly for letting
the hare off.

Visit

BABY PROFESSOR
EDUCATION KIDS

www.BabyProfessorBooks.com

to download Free Baby Professor eBooks
and view our catalog of new and exciting
Children's Books

Made in the USA
Monee, IL
17 April 2021